First Facts™

Why in the World?

What Happened to the Dinosaurs?

A Book about Extinction

by Rebecca Olien

Consultant:
Peter Dodson
Professor of Earth and Environmental Sciences
University of Pennsylvania

Capstone press®
Mankato, Minnesota

First Facts is published by Capstone Press,
151 Good Counsel Drive, P.O. Box 669, Mankato, Minnesota 56002.
www.capstonepress.com

Library of Congress Cataloging-in-Publication Data
Olien, Rebecca.
 What happened to the dinosaurs? : a book about extinction./ by Rebecca Olien.
 p. cm.—(First facts. Why in the world?)
 Includes bibliographical references and index.
 ISBN-13: 978-0-7368-6378-0 (hardcover)
 ISBN-10: 0-7368-6378-8 (hardcover)
 1. Dinosaurs—Extinction—Juvenile literature. I. Title. II. Series.
QE861.6.E95O45 2007
567.9—dc22   2005037718

Summary: A brief explanation of extinction, including what it is, why it happens, and how people
 can help stop it from happening.

Editorial Credits
Jennifer Besel, editor; Juliette Peters, designer; Wanda Winch, photo researcher; Scott Thoms,
 photo editor

Photo Credits
Capstone Press/Karon Dubke, 18
Corbis/Louie Psihoyos, cover (top); Philip Gould, 10
Getty Images Inc./AFP/Ali Burafi, 20; Hulton Archive, 13; Taxi/Ken Lucas, 5;
 Tim Boyle, 4
The Image Works/Syracuse Newspapers/David Lassman, 19
Jon Hughes, 6, 8–9, 12
Minden Pictures/Gerry Ellis, 21; Shin Yoshino, 15
Photodisc/Alan and Sandy Carey, 16
SuperStock/Gary Neil Corbett, cover (bottom)

1 2 3 4 5 6 11 10 09 08 07 06

Table of Contents

Have You Ever Seen a Living Dinosaur?

No one has. Dinosaurs disappeared 65 million years ago. So how do we know they were here? **Fossils** give scientists clues. These ancient bones, eggs, and even footprints tell scientists what lived on earth before us. Maybe you can find fossils in your backyard!

Scientific Inquiry

Making observations and asking questions like the questions in this book are how scientists begin their research. They follow a process known as scientific inquiry.

Ask a Question

Is the ivory-billed woodpecker extinct?

Investigate

The ivory-billed woodpecker had not been seen for 60 years. Then in 2004, researchers heard reports that the bird had been spotted in Arkansas. Using binoculars, video cameras, and recording units, the scientists tried to find this rare bird.

Explain

Some scientists believe they have spotted the ivory-billed woodpecker flying above the trees. They think most of these birds died when much of their forest home was cut down. But thanks to the efforts of a few people, a small part of the forest had been saved. So the ivory-billed woodpecker may still be alive today!

What Happened to the Dinosaurs?

No one knows for sure why the dinosaurs disappeared. Many scientists think an **asteroid** crashed to earth, killing the dinosaurs. The huge rock came from space, moving faster than a rocket. The crash blasted dust into the sky, blocking the sun. It became too cold for the dinosaurs to live.

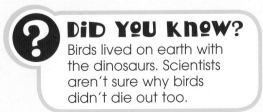

? DID YOU KNOW?
Birds lived on earth with the dinosaurs. Scientists aren't sure why birds didn't die out too.

Other scientists have a different **theory**. They think volcanoes killed the dinosaurs. These volcanoes shot gases into the air. The gases poisoned the water in the air, making rain harmful to plants. When the plants died, the dinosaurs couldn't find enough food to survive.

Could Dinosaurs Ever Come Back?

Dinosaurs are extinct (ek-STINGKT). When an animal is extinct, it's gone forever.

Dinosaurs have been gone for a long time. We will never be able to see a real living dinosaur.

 DID YOU KNOW?
By studying fossils, scientists can tell what a dinosaur ate, how tall it was, and even how fast it could run. Scientists also study fossils and make computer models of what the dinosaur may have looked like.

Have Other Animals Become Extinct?

Millions of animals have come and gone since the beginning of life on earth. The wooly mammoth and saber-toothed tiger went extinct more than 20,000 years ago.

In the 1800s, people hunted the great auk for its meat and feathers. This bird couldn't fly, so it was easy to catch. So many auks were killed that today they are extinct.

Is Extinction Happening Today?

Extinction happens all the time. When people change animal **habitats** by cutting down trees or building roads, animals have a hard time surviving. **Pollution** and overhunting also cause extinction. Many animals, like tigers and blue whales, are **endangered** today. They will become extinct if people don't help them.

DiD YOU KNOW?
Scientists believe there are fewer than 2,500 tigers left in the world. People have changed the tigers' habitat so much, the tigers can't find enough food to eat or a safe place to live.

Why Should I Care about Extinction?

Every animal does a job that helps keep our planet healthy. But when animals go extinct, their job doesn't get done.

Think about the tiny bee. Bees buzz around, **pollinating** plants. But imagine if all the bees disappeared. Plants wouldn't get the pollen they need to make seeds. No seeds would mean fewer fruits or vegetables for us to eat.

What Can I Do to Help?

Ride your bike! Instead of asking mom
to drive you somewhere, ask if you can bike
instead. Cars cause air pollution. Biking helps
stop pollution from killing plants and animals.

The paper we write on each day comes from trees that animals once lived in. Recycling or reusing paper helps save animals' tree homes from being cut down.

The California condor is the largest bird in North America. In 1982, no condors were living in the wild. A few survived in zoos. To save the birds, people kept the condors' eggs safe. When the eggs hatched, people used bird puppets to feed the chicks. Because of this care, more than 200 condors are flying free today.

!

WHAT DO YOU THINK?

Only 1,600 giant pandas are alive today. They live in a few forests in the mountains of China. Pandas are endangered because their forests are being cut down. What do you think can be done to save the giant panda from extinction?

GLOSSARY

asteroid (ASS-tuh-roid)—a large rocky body that moves around the sun

endangered (en-DAYN-jurd)—at risk of dying out

fossil (FOSS-uhl)—the remains or traces of something that once lived; bones and footprints can be fossils.

habitat (HAB-uh-tat)—the place and natural conditions in which plants and animals live

pollinate (POL-uh-nayt)—to move pollen from flower to flower; pollination helps plants make seeds.

pollution (puh-LOO-shuhn)—materials that hurt earth's water, air, and land

theory (THIHR-ee)—an idea that tries to explain something that is unknown

READ MORE

Donald, Rhonda Lucas. *Endangered Animals.* A True Book. New York: Children's Press, 2001.

Eckart, Edana. *California Condor.* Animals of the World. New York: Children's Press, 2003.

Olien, Becky. *Fossils.* Bridgestone Science Library. Mankato, Minn.: Capstone Press, 2002.

INTERNET SITES

FactHound offers a safe, fun way to find Internet sites related to this book. All of the sites on FactHound have been researched by our staff.

Here's how:

1. Visit *www.facthound.com*

2. Choose your grade level.

3. Type in this book ID **0736863788** for age-appropriate sites. You may also browse subjects by clicking on letters, or by clicking on pictures and words.

4. Click on the **Fetch It** button.

FactHound will fetch the best sites for you!

INDEX